WILD WORK

WHO CLEANS DINOSAUR BONES?

WORKING AT A MUSEUM

Margie Markarian

Raintree

www.raintreepublishers.co.uk
Visit our website to find out more information about Raintree books.

To order:
☎ Phone 0845 6044371
▤ Fax +44 (0) 1865 312263
◩ Email myorders@raintreepublishers.co.uk

Customers from outside the UK please telephone +44 1865 312262

Raintree is an imprint of Capstone Global Library Limited, a company incorporated in England and Wales having its registered office at 7 Pilgrim Street, London, EC4V 6LB – Registered company number: 6695582

Edited by David Andrews, Nancy Dickmann, and Rebecca Rissman
Designed by Victoria Allen
Picture research by Liz Alexander
Leveled by Marla Conn, with Read-Ability.
Originated by Dot Gradations Ltd
Printed and bound in China by Leo Paper Products

ISBN 978 1 4062 1676 9 (hardback)
15 14 13 12 11
10 9 8 7 6 5 4 3 2 1

ISBN 978 1 4062 1939 5 (paperback)
16 15 14 13 12
10 9 8 7 6 5 4 3 2 1

British Library Cataloguing in Publication Data
Markarian, Margie.
Who cleans dinosaur bones? : working at a museum. -- (Wild work)
1. Natural history museums--Employees--Juvenile literature.
I. Title II. Series
508'.075-dc22

Acknowledgements
The author and publisher are grateful to the following for permission to reproduce copyright material: Alamy pp. 4 (© Guido Schiefer), 6 (© ilian animal), 7 (© LondonPhotos), 10 (© David R. Frazier Photolibrary, Inc.), 16 (© Kevin Foy), 20 (© imagebroker), 24 (© Luscious Frames), 29 (© Jeff Greenberg); Corbis pp. 5 (© Atlantide Phototravel), 14 (© PHIL McCARTEN), 15 (© HO/Reuters), 18 (© Brooks Kraft), 22 (© Paul A. Souders), 23 (© Jan Butchofsky-Houser), 26 (© Aaron M. Cohen), 27 (© Steve Winter), 28 (© Randy Faris); Getty Images pp. 11 (Jean-Marc Giboux), 12 (Harri Tahvanainen/Gorilla Creative Images), 13 (Matt Cardy), 17 (Chris Jackson), 19 (Tim Graham Photo Library); Photolibrary p. 25 (sodapix/F1 Online); Science Photo Library pp. 8 (Philippe Plailly), 9 (Philippe Plailly); The Colonial Williamsburg Foundation 2008 p. 21 (David M Doody).

Background design features reproduced with permission of Shutterstock (© vgm).

Cover photograph reproduced with permission of Corbis (© Bill Varie).

Contents

Floors to explore

At museums you can go back in time. You can talk to a person from history. You can take a trip to the moon. People who work at museums make all these adventures possible.

DID YOU KNOW?
There are around 2000 museums in Britain.

Collection keepers

Museum **curators** (say *cue-RAY-tors*) are collectors. But they don't collect cuddly toys, trading cards, or action figures.

Some curators collect art or historic items. Others collect scientific objects. They can't put everything they collect on display in the museum at once. They choose items that will interest visitors and teach them new things.

On display

Look at this **hologram**! It welcomes visitors to an **exhibit**, or display, at a science museum in Paris, France.

Exhibit designers create exciting displays like this one. The displays show us why the exhibits are important and how things work. Sometimes the exhibits tell a story.

Who cleans those big bones?

It took 67 million years for this beast to rise again! She is a *Tyrannosaurus rex*, and her name is Sue.

DID YOU KNOW?

A T. Rex could crunch 227 kg (500 lb) of meat in one big bite!

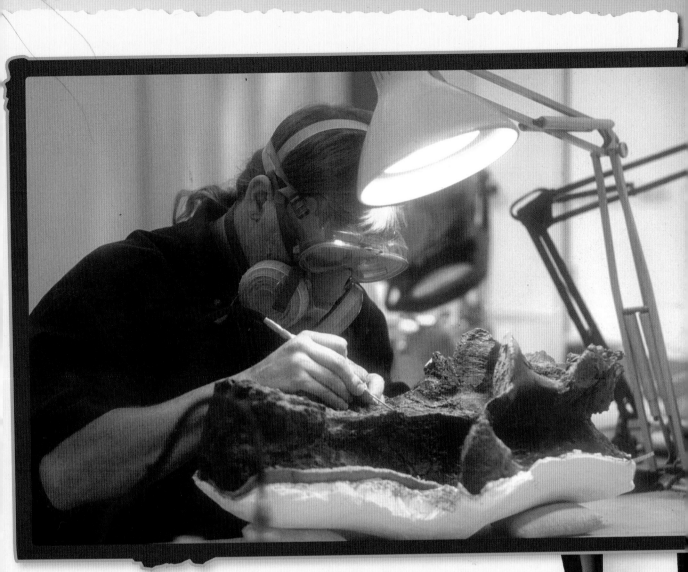

A team of **paleontologists**
(say *PAY-lee-un-TOLL-oh-jists*)
dug Sue's bones out of the
ground. They used special tools
to clean the bones for display.

E..teri..g the de..d zo..e

Watch out! This tiger looks ready to pounce. It seems real because its skin and fur *are* real.

Taxidermists (say *TAX-ee-DURM-ists*) take skin from dead animals. They **preserve,** or save it and use it to make a model. Their work gives people a safe way to learn about animals up close.

Made of wax

Some museums show models of people. They look just like famous people, but they are made of wax!

It takes four months to make one wax figure. Twenty people work together on it. To start, they need photos and more than 250 exact body and face measurements.

To make a head, the team shapes it from a blob of clay. They wait for the clay to harden. The clay face is used to create a **mould**, or a hollow container shaped like the head.

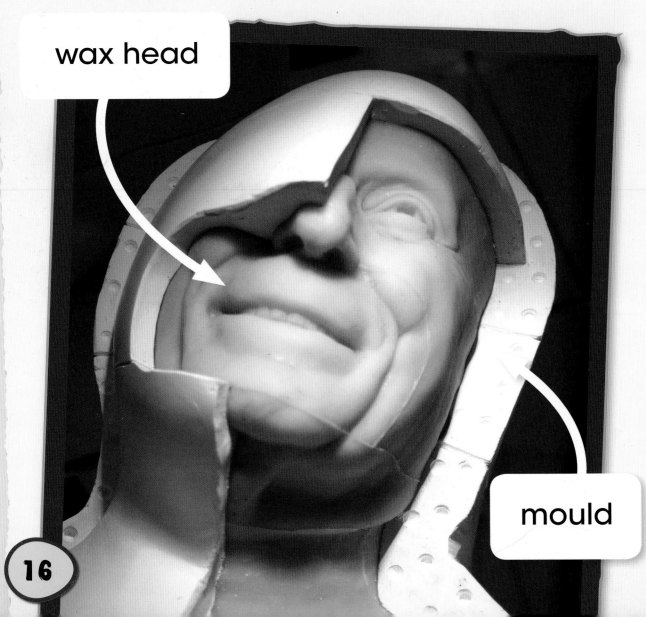

wax head

mould

Hot wax is poured into the mould.
When it cools, it comes out in the
shape of the head. Then it's time
to paint lips, insert hair, and pop
in plastic or glass eyeballs!

Acting the part

At living history museums, workers pretend to be people from the past. They are **role players**.

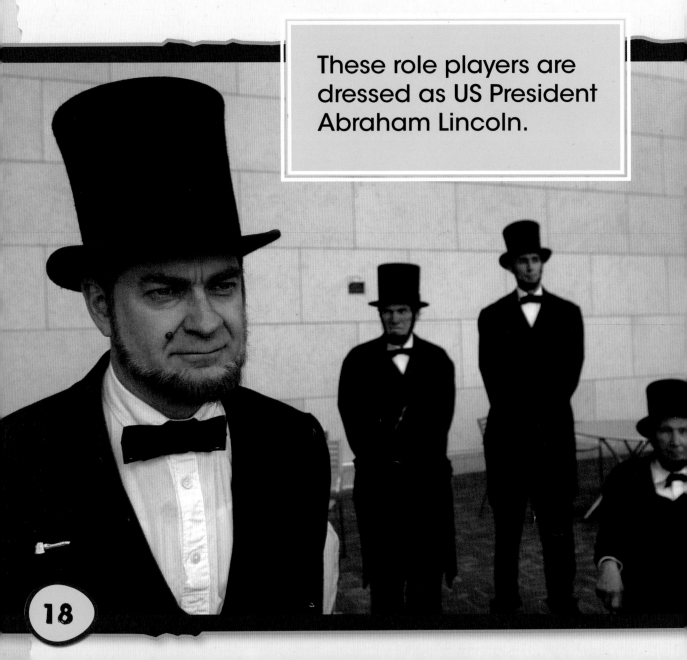

These role players are dressed as US President Abraham Lincoln.

They dress up in costumes and act out history. They show and tell visitors what life was like a long time ago.

Time-travel fashion

Who gives these **role players** something to wear? Costume managers do! Costume managers study fashions from the past. They make sure every button, buckle, and belt fits the time period.

DID YOU KNOW?

The Victoria and Albert Museum in London has one of the largest fashion collections in the world.

Now that's crafty!

Ever wonder how people made food or clothes in the past? They had to work by hand. These museum workers show how crafts were made before machines or factories could make these things for people to buy.

This mans shows how blacksmiths used to make horseshoes.

This woman shows
how fabrics used
to be made.

Sound and light wizards

Audio-visual experts really know how to light up a room. They work to add light and sound to museum **exhibits**. They create lightning bolts in theatres of electricity. They switch on the stars in the night sky at **planetariums**.

A night at the museum

Museums are great places for parties. Special event planners help museums organize parties and other events. Sometimes they arrange sleepovers for schools and families.

These people at New York's Museum of Natural History are sleeping under a blue whale!

Could you work at a museum?

If you love art, history, or science you could work in a museum.

Many museum workers start out as volunteers when they are at school or university. These jobs aren't easy. But they can be a fun way to teach people more about the world.

Glossary

curator person who takes care of
a museum's collections

exhibit a museum display of objects
such as art or historic items

hologram special pattern of lights made to look
like another object

mould hollow container used to shape objects

paleontologists scientists who study the
fossils of living things

planetarium a building with equipment
that can show images from space on
a curved ceiling

preserve save an animal, plant, or object,
usually with chemicals

role player person pretending to be someone else

taxidermist a person who makes stuffed
animals from real animal skins

Find out more

Books to read

Why is Snot Green? The Science Museum Question and Answer Book, Glenn Murphy (Children's Books, 2007)

Websites to visit

http://www.museumsassociation.org/home
The Museums Association has more information about careers in museums.

http://www.nhm.ac.uk/
The Natural History Museum's website has a section for kids with lots of information and games.

http://www.glasgowsciencecentre.org
The Glasgow Science Centre website has games and online experiments for you to try.

http://www.britishmuseum.org/
You can look at thousands of objects in collections from all over the world online on the British Museum's website.

Index